Rose Tobin

THE COMPLETE DRUM TUTOR

Lloyd Ryan

Design by Ashton Christopherson
Illustration by Barbara Griffin www.barbaragriffin.co.uk
Edited by James Ryan and Leo Sutherland

www.thecompletedrumtutor.com

Second edition 1991
Third edition 1996
Fourth edition 2003
Fifth edition 2007
Sixth edition 2013
First published in 1981 by
Gerald Duckworth & Co. Ltd.
The Old Piano Factory
43 Gloucester Crescent, London NW1
© 1981, 1991, 1996, 2003, 2007, 2013 by Lloyd Ryan

Reprinted 2013

ISBN 0 7156 1401 0 paper

British Library Cataloguing in Publication Data
Ryan, Lloyd
The Complete Drum Tutor.
1. Drum
1. Title
789'.1 MT662

ISBN 0-7156-1401-0 Pbk

To buy The Complete Drum Tutor publication, please contact your local music retailer or email: mail@thecompletedrumtutor.com

CONTENTS

PREFACE

One of the problems drummers face when they go to buy a book is which one to buy. There are various books on drumming - on Rock, Jazz, Latin, R&B, Soul, Funk, Hip Hop, Reading, Rudiments, and so on. Therefore to cover every subject they have to buy perhaps five or six books - which can be expensive.
In this book I have tried to include every subject aspiring drummers have to master before they can begin a professional career in music, without including any of the padding - endless pages of the same exercises repeated - so often found in other books.

You may of course - and should - practise the exercises over and over, but the book has been kept to essentials. With careful practice, preferably with a teacher, you should be able to acquire all the skills you need.

Lloyd Ryan

FOREWORD

I've used Lloyd's proven method in The Complete Drum Tutor to teach hundreds of drummers. I've found the concepts in the book to be incredibly effective for all students. The comprehensive content of the book means that once all chapters have been completed, The Complete Drum Tutor continues to act as an invaluable reference for students exploring other areas in the art of drumming. The book's methods also provide the ideal prerequisite for any student planning to take grades.

Here are some testimonies from people who have benefited from learning The Complete Drum Tutor's methods:

"My son has made amazing progress on the drums in a very short period of time. The volume and variety of music taught in 12 months by The Complete Drum Tutor would've taken an average teacher years to impart." - **Gail**

"The Complete Drum Tutor has given me the foundation to be able to pass Trinity Guildhall Drum Kit Grades 1 to 8." - **Thomas**

"I had my doubts about learning to read music. The Complete Drum Tutor made it easy." - **Richard**

To join The Complete Drum Tutor community and hear about drumming workshops, masterclasses and teachers in your area, sign up at: www.thecompletedrumtutor.com and claim a free drum lesson where Lloyd explains the drum score on page 71.

Our aim is to make you... The Complete Drummer.

James Ryan, Founder of The Complete Drum Tutor Collective

INTRODUCTION

ABOUT THE AUTHOR

Lloyd Ryan is regarded as one of the UK's most prolific drum educators with many of his students having gone on to achieve international success. In total, Lloyd's students have recorded 33 Top 10 UK singles and 32 Top 10 UK albums. These include Phil Collins, Derrick McKenzie (Jamiroquai), Graham Broad (Roger Waters, Tina Turner), Ralph Salmins (Robbie Williams, Van Morrison, Björk), John Coghlan (Status Quo) and Nick Simms (Cornershop).
Lloyd has also had his own exciting career spanning four decades. He is widely recognised as an expert of the big band style of drumming, having worked extensively with the Ken Mackintosh, Ray Ellington, Bob Miller and Edmundo Ros Big Bands, as well as major recording artists like Matt Munro, Tony Christie, PJ Proby, Cilla Black, Brotherhood of Man and The Platters.
Lloyd is one of the few UK drummers to have worked alongside the legendary Buddy Rich, as his support act at the Lewisham Jazz Festival in 1986.

"I had lessons with a great drum teacher called Lloyd Ryan. He taught me some really good practice techniques that I still use to this day. Tuition is very important in early stages of playing, especially to develop technique and to play efficiently and effortlessly."
- **Derrick McKenzie** (Jamiroquai)

"I went to Lloyd Ryan, he was fantastic."
- **Graham Broad** (Roger Waters, Tina Turner, Bill Wyman)

"When I was 16, Ken Mackintosh, my first band leader/employer said to me: "Go and see Lloyd Ryan; he will show you how to hit the drums"...and he did!"
- **Ralph Salmins** (Robbie Williams, Van Morrison, Björk)

"I used to watch Lloyd Ryan play. I thought he was a great drummer and he taught me."
- **John Coghlan** (Status Quo)

"Lloyd Ryan taught me to read music, he also taught me to play as part of a band and not just as a solo player. He taught me that although the main point is that you're keeping time, you also have to fit in melodically with everything that's going on in the band, not just with the bass player. I don't know if he realises that he does that - it's something in the way he teaches. Like if you're studying a drum part, when you get to play it with a recording, feel is the thing you want – so once he's got you though the basics of technique and reading, he concentrates on getting the feel right, rather than just playing the part like a robot."
- **Nick Simms** (Cornershop)

"On behalf of the British drum community, you've influenced us, or you've taught someone who has influenced us. Your drumming DNA is floating around all over the UK."
- **Ian Croft** (iDrum Magazine)

THE COMPLETE DRUM TUTOR COLLECTIVE

The Complete Drum Tutor Collective is a group of tutors who use Lloyd's proven method of teaching as shown in this book. The concepts, explanations and exercises provide the perfect foundation for students planning to take grades – and also for those looking to expand their studies into different styles with other educational material available.

For more information regarding Lloyd Ryan masterclasses,
The Complete Drum Tutor Collective workshops & lessons,
email: mail@thecompletedrumtutor.com

1. KEEPING TIME

'Time conquers all, and we must time obey'
- **Alexander Pope**

The word 'time' in music does not mean the time you tell from a clock, it refers to keeping time or tempo. A drummer's job is to keep tempo. For example, if a band or group leader counts you in 1, 2, 3, 4, your job is to maintain that speed, whatever it may be. To help you practise, buy a metronome. When practising the exercises in this book, always play them slowly at first. Never speed up as you go along. If you wish to play them faster, stop and then count yourself in at the new tempo.

2. THE STAVE

The stave ≡≡≡ consists of five horizontal lines close together, on which the notes are written, with vertical bar lines to separate the bars.

The number of beats in each bar depends on the time in which the music is written.

Thus $\frac{4}{4}$ time, or Common Time, contains four beats in each bar and $\frac{3}{4}$ time contains three beats.

Ordinary sheet music written for Piano has two staves, the upper stave bearing the sign of the Treble Clef 𝄞 and the lower stave the sign of the Bass Clef 𝄢. Drum music is usually written in the Bass Clef, on a single stave.

The sign ‖: followed later by :‖ indicates that the passage in between is to be repeated.

3. NOTES AND THEIR TIME VALUES

The range of notes and their relative values may be set out as follows, as they would appear in Common Time:

whole note (semi-breve)

half note (minim)

quarter note (crotchet)

eighth note (quaver)

sixteenth note (semi-quaver) j

thirty-second note (demi-semi-quaver)

A grace note is a note without specific time value played very softly just before a proper note.

N.B. (a) As shorthand, groups of four thirty-second notes (demi-semi-quavers) are often written ♪ or ♪♪♪♪ etc., see page 45.
(b) For rests, see page 17.
(c) For tied notes, see page 30.
(d) For dotted notes, see page 33.

4. TIME SIGNATURES

The time signature at the beginning of a piece of music tells you the time in which the piece is written. It consists usually of two figures, one above the other, $\frac{4}{4}$, $\frac{3}{4}$, $\frac{6}{8}$ etc., the bottom figure signifying the *value* of the note which is the unit of time and the top figure the *number* of such units in each bar.

Thus $\frac{4}{4}$ means that there are 4 quarter notes (crotchets) in each bar, $\frac{3}{4}$ that there are 3 quarter notes (crotchets) in each bar, $\frac{3}{8}$ that there are 3 eighth notes (quavers) in each bar, and so on.

Common Time $\frac{4}{4}$ is often indicated by the symbol **C**.

Basically, music is in either *double* or *triple* time, according to whether the number of beats in the bar is divisible by 2 or 3.

A beat in double or triple time may itself consist of a triplet

N.B. The word 'beat' is here used in its general musical sense of one of the fixed number of beats in a bar. This must not be confused with the sense in which drummers often also use the word, namely as the beat of a drumstick, whether or not the note falls on one of the regular beats of a bar.

5. DYNAMICS

The letter *p* (*piano*) signifies that a note or passage has to be played softly (*pp* , *pianissimo* = very softly), *f* (*forte*) that it must be played loud (*ff* , *fortissimo* = very loud).

The sign ———————— (*crescendo*) denotes gradually increasing volume and ———————— (*diminuendo*) gradually decreasing volume.
The sign > above a note ♩ indicates that it is accented.

6. DRUM NOTES

Each drum part has a different line or space. The commonest notation, used in this book , is as follows:

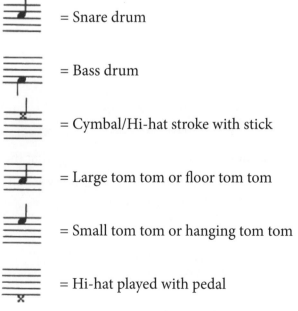

= Snare drum

= Bass drum

= Cymbal/Hi-hat stroke with stick

= Large tom tom or floor tom tom

= Small tom tom or hanging tom tom

= Hi-hat played with pedal

7. HOW TO HOLD THE DRUMSTICKS

Traditional grip (also known as orthodox grip)

Matched grip

www.thecompletedrumtutor.com

8. HOW TO PLAY WITH THE FOOT

(a) The bass drum

(i) Played with the foot flat on the pedal

(ii) Played with the toe

(b) The hi-hat

N.B. If you are left-handed or left-footed, reverse these instructions, i.e. left foot bass drum, right foot hi-hat.

9. TUNING THE DRUM SET

Snare drum (Rock/Country)
For rock or country music you need a flat sound. This is obtained by slackening the top head and applying gaffer tape or a sticky gel such as RTOM's Moongel to it. The amount you use depends on the sound you want. To start with, use a piece of gaffer tape approximately 4" (10cm long – or one piece of sticky gel) and add as required.

Snare drum (Jazz)
For jazz you need a brighter, livelier sound. This is obtained by tightening both heads. Tighten the top head so that you can just about press the head inwards with your thumb, and then tighten the bottom head one degree more than the top.

Bass drum (Rock/Country/Recording)
Most drummers take the front head off and then put a cloth or small blanket inside, making sure that the material touches the playing head.

Bass drum (Jazz style)
For jazz style you would most certainly leave the front head on, but it is useful to put a felt strip on each head (on the inside) from top to bottom.

Tom toms (Rock/Country /Recording)
Many drummers take the bottom head off and again apply gaffer tape or sticky gel pieces to each drum as required. This is the method I would use if I were recording or being mic'd into a 'P.A.' system. But if I were playing in a small area 'un-mic'd' I would leave both heads on and tune as for the jazz-style snare drum, making sure that the small tom tom sounds higher in pitch than the large. This, however, is a matter for personal preference and experimentation.

**WHENEVER YOU SEE THIS ILLUSTRATION
THE FOLLOWING EXERCISES ARE ESSENTIAL FOR LEARNING.**

"Inspiration exists, but it has to find you working."
- Pablo Picasso

Good luck working through The Complete Drum Tutor.
Your drumming journey starts here. We'll be with you every step of the
way – sign up with us at: **www.thecompletedrumtutor.com** to let us
help find the best drum teacher for you.

On the website you'll also be able to claim a free classic drum track
and lesson.

Remember there is plenty of room at the top.

CHAPTER 1: READING EXERCISES

'If you wish to reach the highest, begin at the lowest'
- Publilius Syrus

Really work hard on these first 3 sets of exercises, they are not easy to begin with. However once mastered, they will help you gain the independence between all of your limbs that you will need to become a complete drummer.

'If it doesn't challenge you, it won't change you.'

1. Quarter notes (crotchets)

2. Eighth notes (quavers)

www.thecompletedrumtutor.com

3. Sixteenth notes (semi-quavers)

Single stroke roll

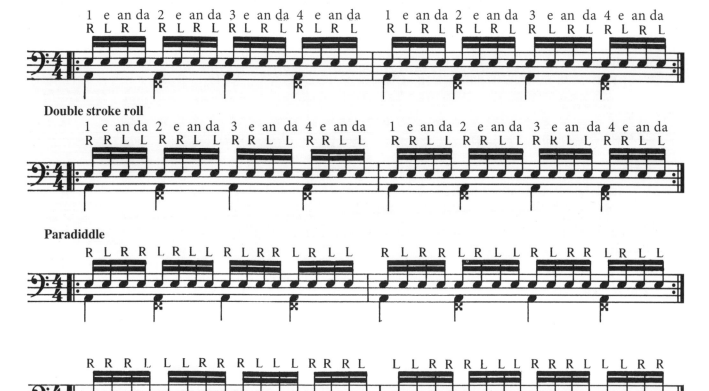

In the following exercise, A1 and B1 are bars of sixteenth notes (semi-quavers) with four sixteenth notes (semi-quavers) to the beat; but in A2 each beat consists of an eighth note (quaver) followed by two sixteenth notes (semi-quavers), and in B2 of two sixteenth notes (semi-quavers) followed by an eighth note (quaver). Study this exercise carefully, because these rhythms recur frequently later.

4. Thirty-second notes (demi-semi-quavers)

Single stroke roll

Double stroke roll

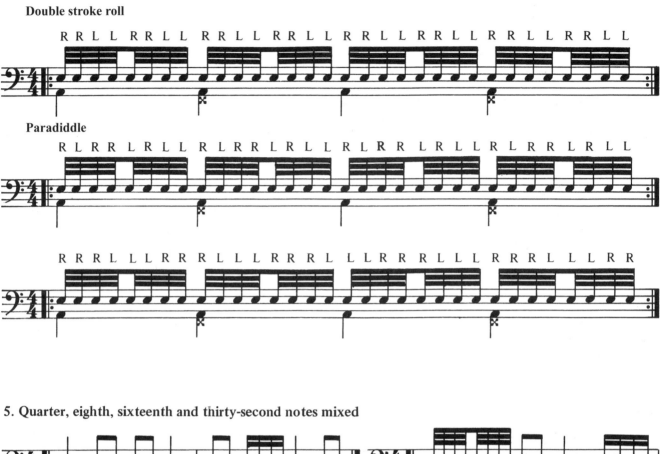

Paradiddle

5. Quarter, eighth, sixteenth and thirty-second notes mixed

6. Rests

A rest means silence. For each note there exists a rest of equivalent value.

* Whole note (Semi-breve)	Half note (Minim)	Quarter note (Crotchet)	Eighth note (Quaver)	Sixteenth note (Semi-quaver)	Thirty-second note (Demi-semi-quaver)

*The whole note rest is also used to show one complete bar of silence irrespective of the number of beats in the bar.

(a) Quarter-note (crotchet) rest

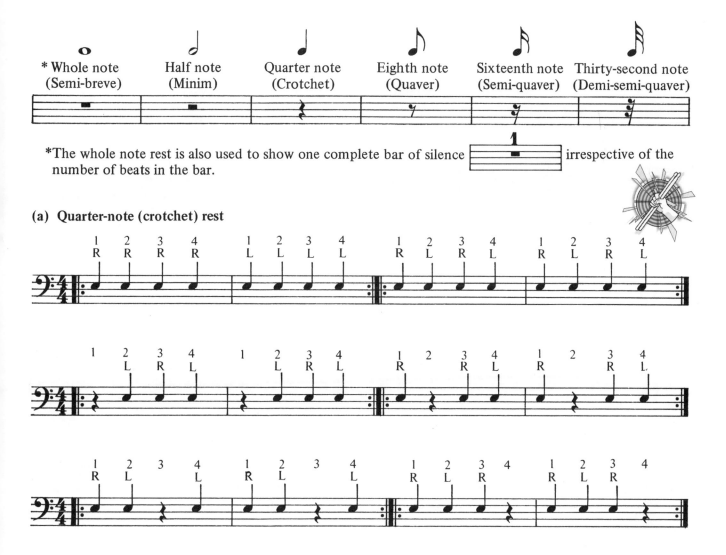

(b) **Eighth-note (quaver) rest**

(c) Sixteenth-note (semi-quaver) rest

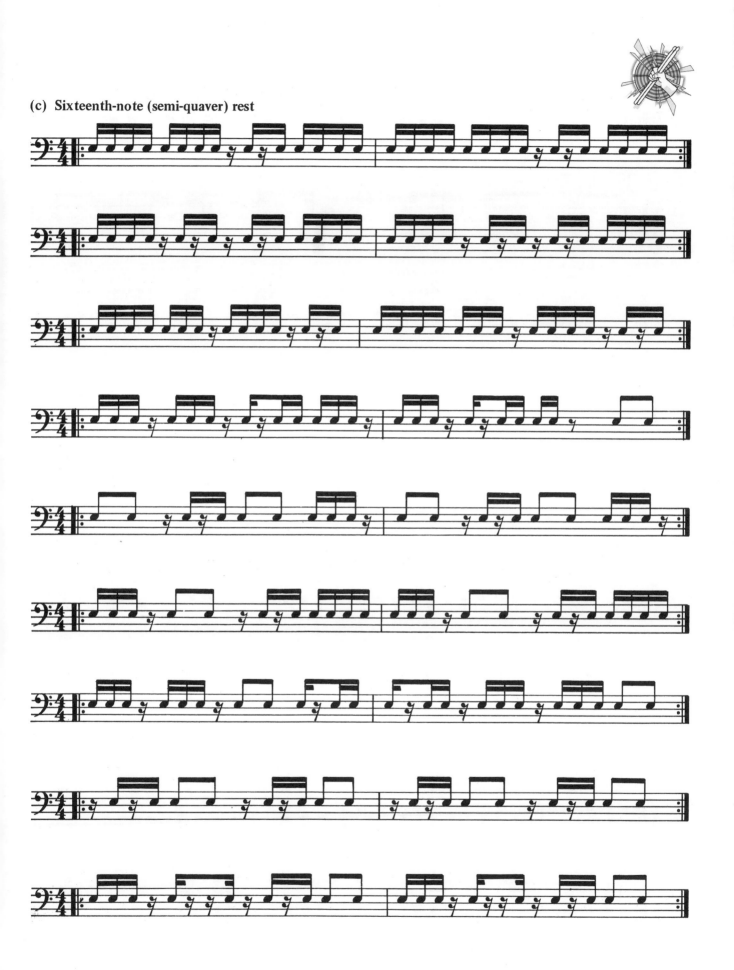

(d) Thirty-second-note (demi-semi-quaver) rest

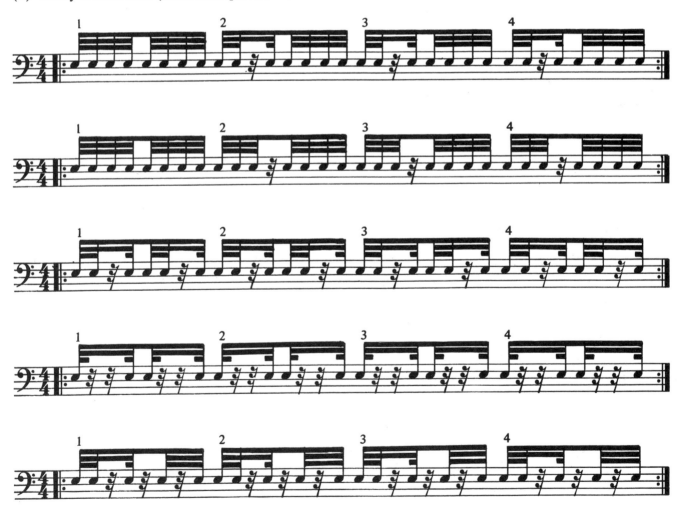

7. $\frac{3}{4}$ time

The following exercises in $\frac{3}{4}$ time incorporate the bass drum and hi-hat.

8. Triplets

Triplets are groups of three. There are 12 eighth-note (quaver) triplets to one bar of $\frac{4}{4}$ time.

(a) Eighth-note (quaver) triplets

(b) Triplets with accents

An accent > above a note indicates that it must be played at twice the volume.

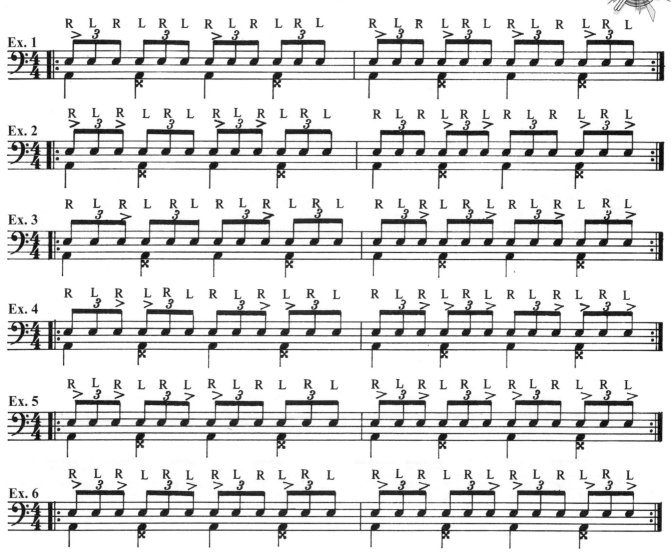

(c) Triplets with tom tom accents

Ex. 1

Ex. 2

Ex. 3

Ex. 4

Ex. 5

Ex. 6

(d) Triplets incorporating bass drum
(Use hand to hand stickings, i.e. LRLR or RLRL)

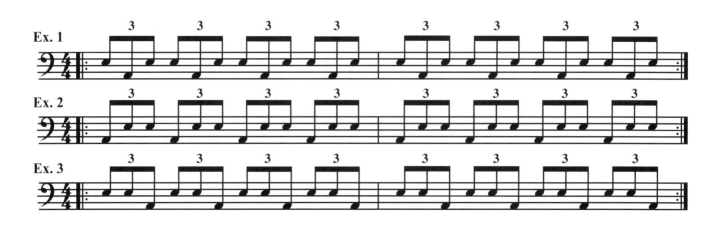

Ex. 1

Ex. 2

Ex. 3

Ex. 4

Ex. 5

Ex. 6

Ex. 7

(e) Quarter-note (crotchet) triplets
There are 6 quarter-note (crotchet) triplets to one bar of $\frac{4}{4}$ time.

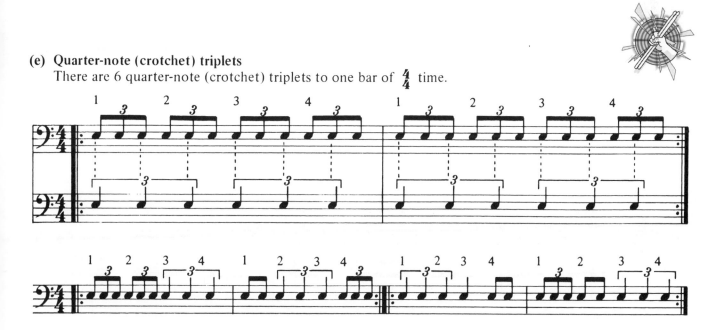

www.thecompletedrumtutor.com

(f) Sixteenth-note (semi-quaver) triplets

There are 24 sixteenth-note (semi-quaver) triplets to one bar of $\frac{4}{4}$ time.

(g) Eighth-note (quaver) triplets containing sixteenth notes (semi-quavers)

9. Tied notes

A tied note ♩‿♩ is one that continues the tone of the previous note. In drumming, because there is no continuous tone, a tied note is equivalent to a rest, *i.e.* only the first of two tied notes is played.

www.thecompleteddrumtutor.com

10. Whole notes (semi-breves) and half notes (minims)

(a) Exercises with half notes (minims)

(b)   Exercises with both whole notes (semi-breves) and half notes (minims)

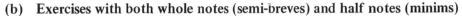

11.   Whole-note (semi-breve) rests and half-note (minim) rests

12. Dotted notes

A dot after a note makes that note half as long again, or increases its value by half.

Exercises using dotted eighth notes (quavers), dotted quarter notes (crotchets) and dotted half notes (minims)

13. Dynamics

Try the following simple exercise and see how by observing the dynamics you improve the sound.

14. A twelve-bar solo with dynamics

www.thecompletedrumtutor.com

15. Syncopation

A shifting of the usual rhythmic accent by stressing the normally unaccented beats.
The easiest way to practise is to count up to eight as in Ex.1

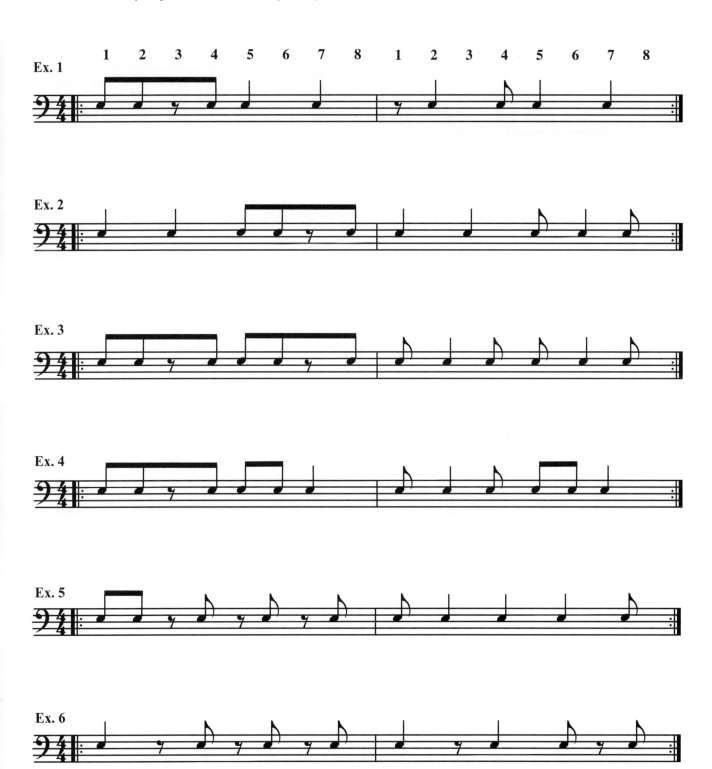

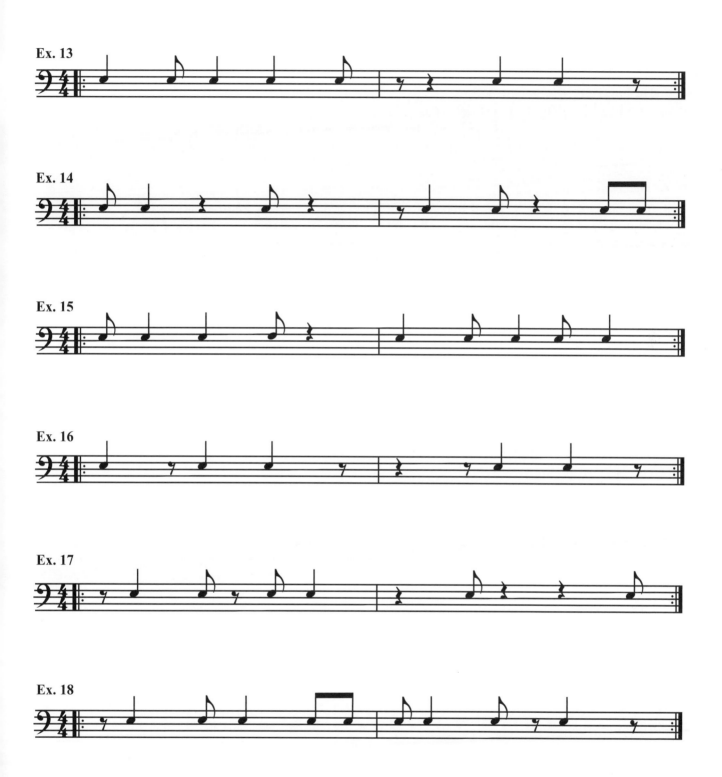

1. The Standard 26 American Drum Rudiments

All rudiments are to be played open *(slow)* and close *(fast)*

No. 1. The long roll

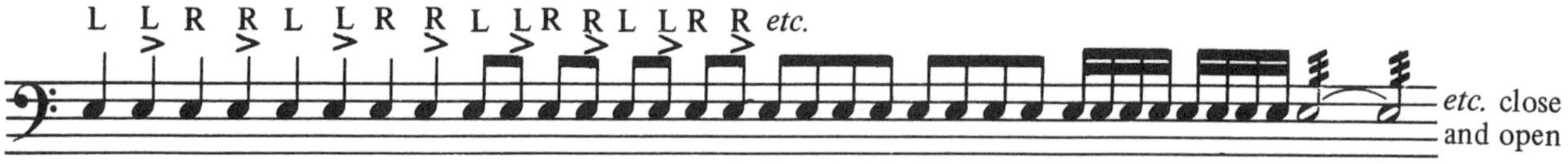

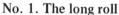

No. 2. The 5-stroke roll

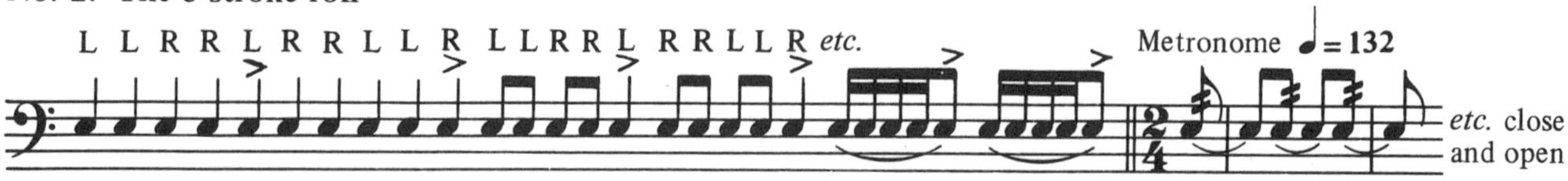

No. 3. The 7-stroke roll

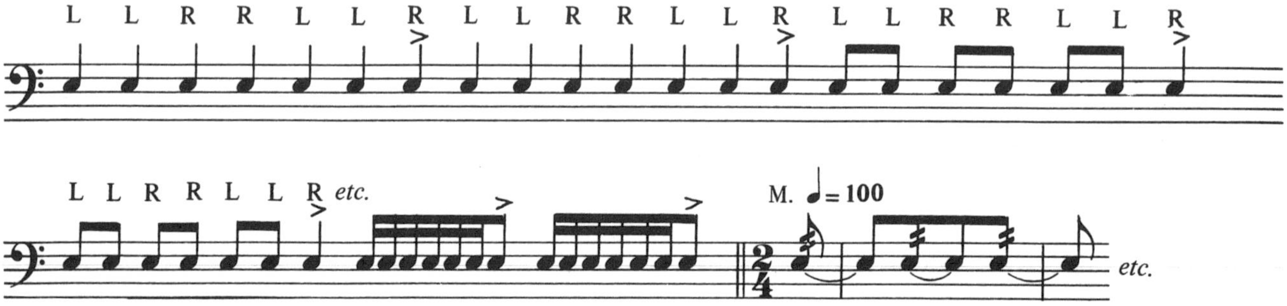

No. 4. The flam

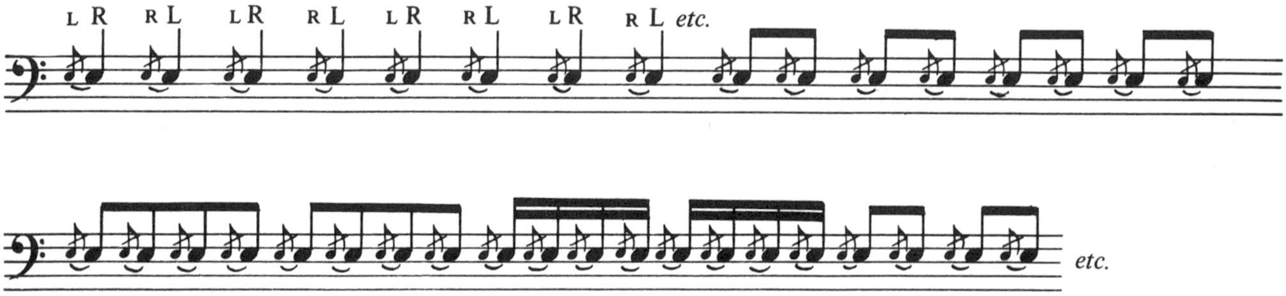

No. 5. The flam accent

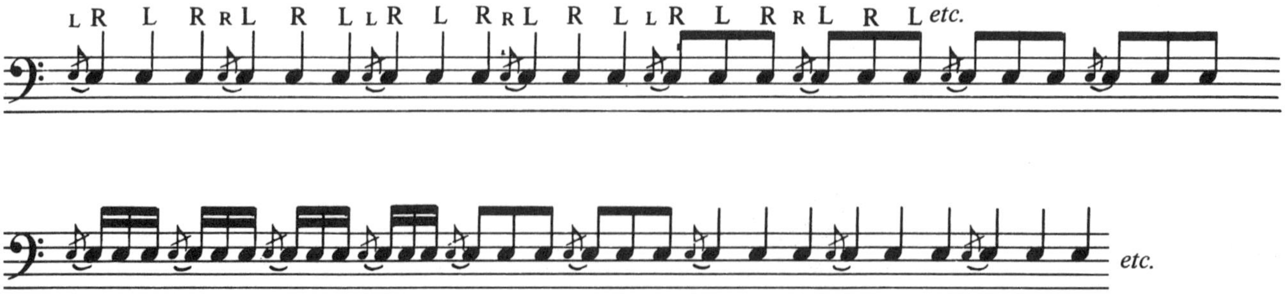

No. 6. The flam paradiddle

No. 7. The flamacue

No. 8. The drag

No. 9. The single drag

No. 10. The double drag

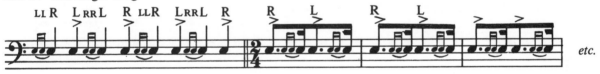

No. 11. The double paradiddle

No. 12. The single ratamacue

No. 13. The triple ratamacue

No. 14. The single-stroke roll

No. 15. The 9-stroke roll

No. 16. The 10-stroke roll

No. 17. The 11-stroke roll

No. 18. The 13-stroke roll

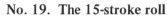

No. 19. The 15-stroke roll

No. 20. The flam tap

L R   R rL   L lR   R rL   L lR RrL LlR RrL L *etc.*

No. 21. The single paradiddle

L R L L R L R R   LRLLRLRR LRLLRLRR

No. 22. The drag paradiddle no. 1

R L L R L R R L R R L R L L R LLRLRRL RRLRLLR llRLRR

etc

No. 23. The drag paradiddle no. 2

R L L R L L R L R R L R R L R R L R L L

No. 24. The flam paradiddle-diddle

L R L R R L L R L R L L R RrLRLRRLLrLRLLRR *etc.*

No. 25. Lesson 15

L L R L R L L R L R L L R L R L L R L R

(inverted)

No. 26. The double ratamacue

L L R L L R L R L R R L R R L R L R

2. Single-stroke roll

The single-stroke roll is so named because you play single beats, *i.e.* RL RL RL *etc.*

3. Long roll (Dadda Mamma)

This is one of the most famous rudiments in drumming, known as the 'Dadda Mamma' for its sound.

The long roll would be written the following way in a band arrangement or marching band part:

4. Paradiddles

(a) Single paradiddle

(b) Double paradiddle (in triplet form)

(c) Triple paradiddle

(d) Reverse paradiddle

(e) Inward paradiddle

(f) Single paradiddle in triplet form

5. Paradiddles with accents

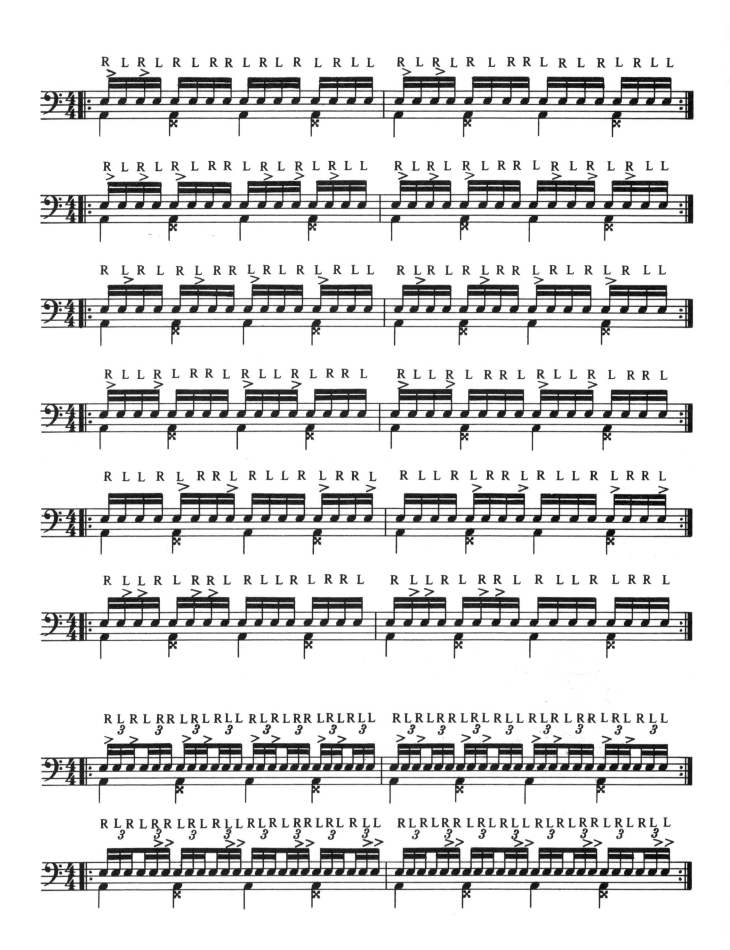

6. Para-rock

These exercises make good Rock beats

7. Press roll

Many drummers confuse the long roll with the press roll. The long roll always remains RR LL RR LL. The press roll consists of single beats RL RL RL RL, but each stick is then allowed to bounce as many times as it can on the head of the drum. With practice a continuous roll develops.

Press roll exercises

www.thecompletedrumtutor.com

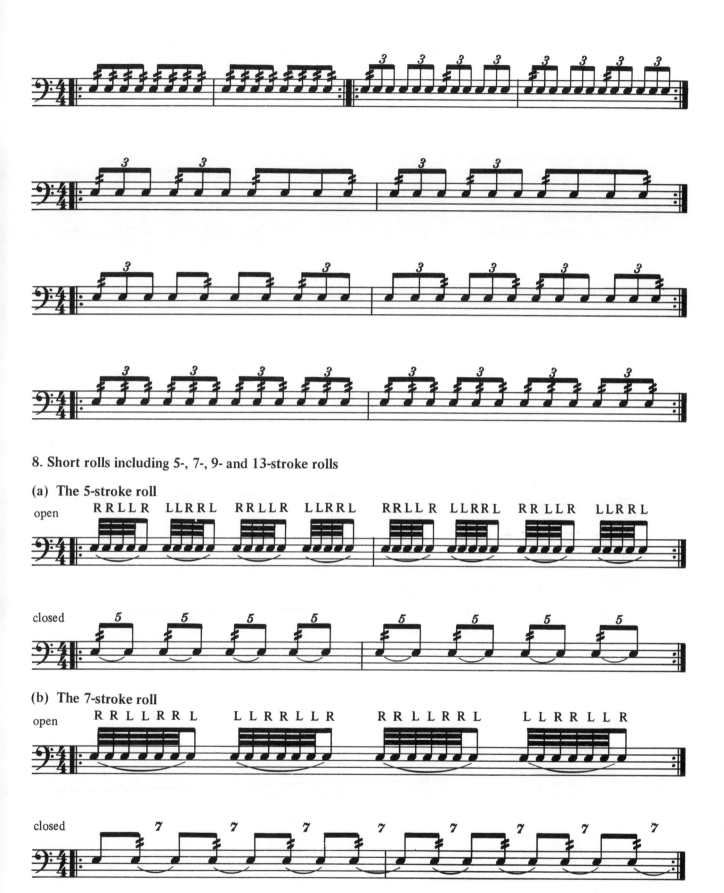

8. Short rolls including 5-, 7-, 9- and 13-stroke rolls

(a) The 5-stroke roll

open

RRLLR   LLRRL   RRLLR   LLRRL   RRLLR   LLRRL   RRLLR   LLRRL

closed

(b) The 7-stroke roll

open

RRLLRRL   LLRRLLR   RRLLRRL   LLRRLLR

closed

(c) The 9-stroke roll

(d) The 13-stroke roll

9. Basic snare drum rudiments

(a) The flam

(b) The drag

(c) The ratamacue
A drag before a triplet

(i) single ratamacue

(ii) double ratamacue

(iii) triple ratamacue

(d) The ruff

Two, three or four grace notes are followed by a normal beat.

(i) 3-stroke ruff

(ii) 4-stroke ruff

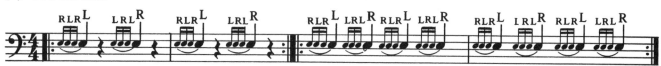

(iii) 5-stroke ruff

(e) Flam paradiddle

(f) Drag paradiddles

10. Accented notes

(a) Sixteenth notes (semi-quavers) / eighth notes (quavers)

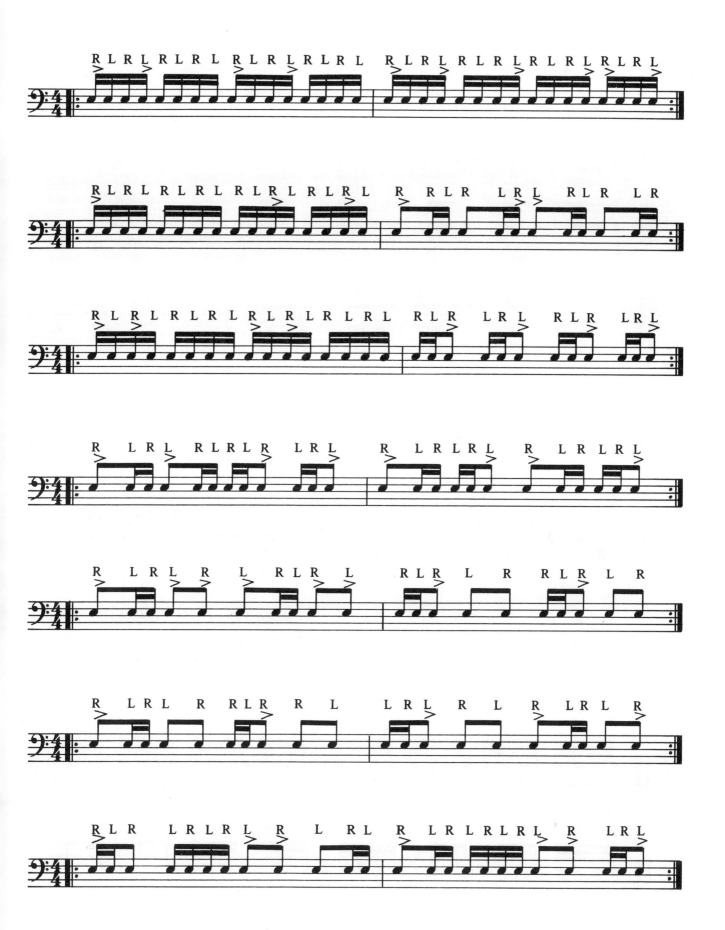

(b) Sixteenth notes (semi-quavers) / eighth notes (quavers) with bass drum accents

(c) Thirty-second notes (demi-semi-quavers)

www.thecompletedrumtutor.com

11. Miscellaneous

(a) Bars which sound the same, though the second is written differently from the first

(b) Triplets with unusual sticking (ideal for playing around the kit)

CHAPTER 3: ROCK, JAZZ FUNK, JAZZ AND WORLD GROOVES

Remember: practise each exercise slowly at first, gradually increasing speed over a period of several weeks.

Before beginning the exercises, practise the following rhythms carefully.

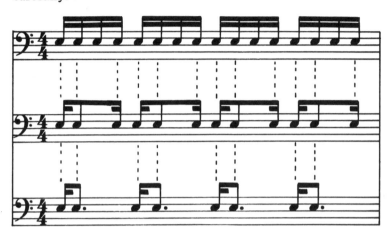

1. Rock

(a) Preliminary

(b) Eighth notes (quavers)

These exercises are suitable for Rock, pop and country style playing.

Ex. 1

Ex. 2

Ex. 3

Ex. 4

Ex. 5

Ex. 6

(c) Eighth notes (quavers) with open hi-hat
(0 = open)

Ex. 7

Ex. 8

Ex. 9

Ex. 10

Ex. 11

Ex. 12

(d) Sixteenth notes (semi-quavers)

(e) Sixteenth notes (semi-quavers) and sixteenth-note (semi-quaver) triplets

2. Jazz funk

3. Jazz

The basic difference between Rock drumming and Jazz drumming is that with Rock, the basic metre is

And with Jazz it is

Again, practise slowly at first, increasing speed over a period of several weeks. It may also help you to play along with Jazz recordings.

(a) Quarter-note (crotchet), eighth-note (quaver) and sixteenth-note (semi-quaver) triplets

Ex. 1

Ex. 2

Ex. 3

Ex. 4

Ex. 5

Ex. 6

(b) Exercises using snare drum and bass drum

Ex. 7

Ex. 8

Ex. 9

Ex. 10

Ex. 11

4. World grooves

There are countless rhythms from all around the world, and below we've shown a small selection of the more popular ones. After you have practised these grooves, find some recordings in these styles and try to play along with them to get the right feel.

(a) Bossa Nova

(b) Quick Step

(c) Tango

(d) Pasa Doble

(e) Samba

(f) Rhumba

(g) Cha Cha

www.thecompletedrumtutor.com

(h) Beguine

(i) Mambo

(j) Samba No.2 in four

(k) Waltz (brushes)

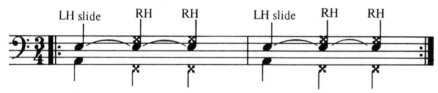

(l) Songo

(m) Merengue

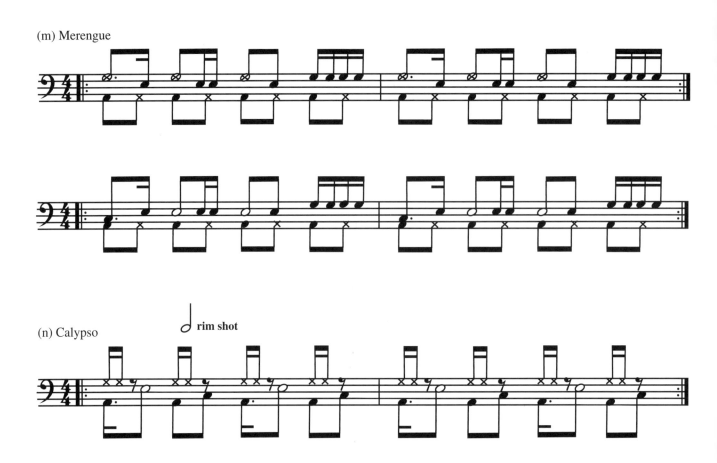

(n) Calypso

♩ rim shot

CHAPTER 4: DRUM SCORES

Scores are not always printed but can be written by hand.
The parts which follow are examples of what you might find.

Note the first- and second-time bars (1° and 2°) in lines 4 and 5. These show that there is a variation at the end when the section is played a second time.

Note also the sign 𝄋 (*Dal Segno* = 'back to the sign') indicated in lines 2 and 12, and the sign ⊕ marked 'Coda' ('tailpiece') in lines 3 and 13. At the end of line 12 you go back to the sign at the beginning of line 2. When you reach the sign 'To ⊕' in line 3 you jump to the Coda.

SKINS   BIG SWING FACE

A free drum lesson where Lloyd explains how you could approach this part is available at: **www.thecompletedrumtutor.com**

Lloyd plays a version of this part on his big band album, 'Drivin' Force' available on iTunes and Amazon

CHAPTER 5: SOLOS, DUETS AND A TRIO

1. Two-, four-, eight-, twelve-, sixteen-bar solos

(a) Two-bar solos using triplets, sixteenth notes (semi-quavers), small tom tom and large tom tom

(b) Four-bar solos using sixteenth notes (semi-quavers) and sixteenth-note (semi-quaver) rests

Ex. 5

(c) Eight-bar solos using dotted eighth notes (quavers), triplets and sixteenth notes (semi-quavers)

Ex. 1

Ex. 2

(d) Twelve-bar solos in Jazz, Latin and Rock rhythms, using all the drums and cymbals

Ex. 1

Ex. 2

(e) Sixteen-bar solo using full kit

www.thecompletedrumtutor.com

2. Two duets by Lloyd Ryan

(a) Two's Company

The first drummer plays snare drum with snares on throughout the
solo. The second drummer uses tom toms and snare drum with
snares off to make an extra tom tom effect.

(b) Triplets for Two

Snare drum

Tom tom &
bass drum

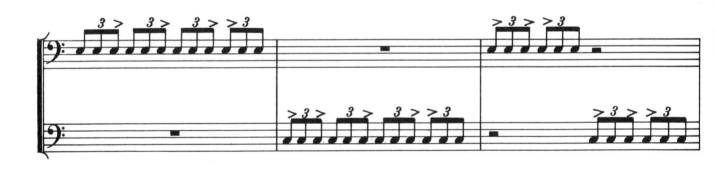

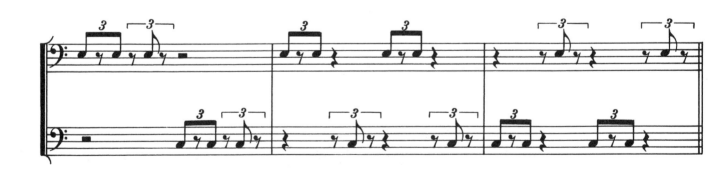

www.thecompletedrumtutor.com

3. A trio by Lloyd Ryan

Three's a Crowd

CHAPTER 6: ODD TIME SIGNATURES

1. **Exercises using** $\frac{5}{4}$, $\frac{7}{4}$, $\frac{9}{4}$ **time**

As in $\frac{4}{4}$ time the unit is still the quarter note (crotchet). In a $\frac{5}{4}$ bar there are 5 quarter notes (crotchets) or 10 eighth notes (quavers); in a $\frac{7}{4}$ bar 7 quarter notes (crotchets) or 14 eighth notes (quavers); in a $\frac{9}{4}$ bar 9 quarter notes (crotchets) or 18 eighth notes (quavers).

(a) $\frac{5}{4}$ time

(b) A four-bar Jazz solo in $\frac{5}{4}$ time

(c) $\frac{7}{4}$ time

(d) A four-bar Rock break in $\frac{7}{4}$ time

(e) $\frac{9}{4}$ time

(f) A four-bar solo in $\frac{9}{4}$ time

2. Exercises using eighth notes (quavers) as the basic unit

The difference between $\frac{3}{8}$ and $\frac{3}{4}$ time is that in $\frac{3}{8}$ time a bar consists of three eighth notes (quavers) and in $\frac{3}{4}$ time of three quarter notes (crotchets). $\frac{3}{8}$ time tends to be faster than $\frac{3}{4}$ time. $\frac{6}{8}$, $\frac{9}{8}$ and $\frac{12}{8}$ (known as compound time) have the same triple rhythm as $\frac{3}{8}$ time, but with two, three and four times the number of triplets in each bar. In $\frac{5}{8}$, $\frac{7}{8}$, $\frac{10}{8}$ and $\frac{11}{8}$ time, a bar consists of 5, 7, 10 and 11 eighth-note (quaver) beats respectively, each beat having the same value.

3. Rhythms using odd time signatures ideal for Latin or Jazz beats

Ex. 1

Ex.1(a) Rhythmic example (Mambo in 6)

Ex. 2

Ex. 2(a) Rhythmic example (Greek 9 – 2+2+2+3)

Ex. 3

Ex. 3(a) Rhythmic example

The following three exercises are useful rhythmic variations in $\frac{5}{8}$, $\frac{6}{8}$ and $\frac{11}{8}$.

Ex. 4

Ex. 5 (Mambo/African $\frac{6}{8}$)

Ex. 6 (African $\frac{11}{8}$)

Solo using $\frac{3}{8}$, $\frac{5}{8}$ and $\frac{11}{8}$

For extra study, try to obtain percussion parts from works by twentieth-century composers such as Stravinsky, Berg, Maxwell Davies, Stockhausen and so on. Most public libraries which loan music have study scores of various modern works. From these you can study the percussion parts while listening to the recordings.

I hope you have found this book useful, and that it will be the first step in a successful and enjoyable venture or career in the music world. Remember, *practice makes perfect*, and in the words of Edison:

'Genius is one percent inspiration and ninety-nine percent perspiration.'